IS/

I HAVE A WORD

PSALMS OF THE PANDEMIC

To Rosalinda

Where am I am from //
From my mother's womb? 1
Isaac K.

"The major problem of life is learning how,
 to handle the costly interruptions.
The door that slams shut the plan that was sidetracked,
 the marriage that failed.
 Or that lovely power that didn't get written,
  because someone knocked on the door."

Rev. Dr. Martin Luther King Jr.

"Poet you shall speak,
You that the gods have
elected; That sings songs; our
sources That vibrates sieves;
our forest That arid be
grassy…"

Jacques Rabemanadjara

1. I HAVE A WORD

I have a word,
like a sachet of golden diamonds.
I have a word for the orphan.
I have a word for the widower.
I have a word,
like a cloth oily perfumed.
I have verbs in my soul that recite and testify.
I have a word for the marginalized.
I have a word for the poor.

Those tough times do not always mean bad times.
That if you can win, you can convince someone.
That if you are the last to be helped, be the first to help.
Let not your circumstance determine your time,
but let your time determine your circumstance.

I have a word for the immigrants crossing the river.
I have a word for the weak on the bed of death.
I have a word for the soldiers battling to protect us. I
have a word for the prisoners in the cells of detention.

That the wind of the east and the breeze of the plain are still blowing.

That the bird of the valley and the eagle of the mountain are still in motion.

That the flower and the herb will find enough water to flourish.
As the sun will shine in the morning and the moon by night,
the earth still rotates and no one can stop its motion.

My word is - nobody knows the future.
My word is - living is moving.
My word is - waiting is working.
My word is - it is just a matter of time.
My word is - everything in this world is a word.
My word is - if you can define it, you can find it.
My word is - what was impossible yesterday is possible today.
My word is - what is impossible today will be possible tomorrow.
My word is - your life is a mission and your mission is possible.

A healthy relationship will start with these words,

"I have no gold or silver for you but plenty of time to offer you."

2 WALKING THE ROAD

Albert walked here.
With his mind, he walked.
I mean the great Albert Einstein.
He paved my road; he discovered the theory. His
relativity vision set a standard for me. For a time
such as this, he teaches me. He teaches me to
walk the road, even in the cold.

Rosa walked here,
By foot, she did yes, and she marched.
I mean the queen, Rosa Parks.
She drove my ride.
Her equal seat established mine.
For the slow motion, she sighted me.
I can feel her, driving beside me.

Mohamed walked here.
I mean the great Mohamed Ali.
He punched my chains down.
I prayed at his jungle-rumbled site.
He pulled me out of my stumbles.
"Ali boom yea," I am still praising him.
From the rings of his corners, he coached me.

Jonathan preached here.
I mean Jonathan Edwards, the preacher.
By his altar, I am learning and praying
the standards of holiness he set,
the cannons of morals, he drafted.
The preacher is challenging my standard.
I am facing greatness in ministry.

Martin Luther King spoke here.
I mean the dream personified, stood here.
I cannot ask for better than this.
I am walking the road of his greatness,
the sound of his lengthy diction calling.
I will be judge not by the long road I took,
but by the road he walked before me.

Westbrook, Maine. September 27, 2017

The cross of a visionary is that the past rejected you, the present ignores you, and the future will miss you.

9

3 CROSSING THE RIVER

Eagle, cross me your river since
my wings have weakened.
Little bird, take me to your nest.
I shall then believe what I see.
I shall sing in your harmony.

Falcon, baptize me in your river
since my skin has vanished.
Eagle, tell me about Luther King.
I shall then live to believe. I shall
meditate on his dream.

Engine, push me over the canyons
since my soul needs your counsel.
Rotors fly me upon the oceans.

I shall not sink to perish.
I shall then live among the free.

4 LESSER IS GREAT

The minus is greater.
Diminishing is just perception.
Nothing is bigger than any.
Nothing is inferior to yours.
Lesser is greater.
The miniature is wonderful.

The smaller is the sense.
Greater is the sensibility.
The wholeness of life is in the
least. Dive into smaller,
the higher your perception becomes.

When least you sense
Inner sensors open wide
Confined is your greatness
In the less you navigate quickly

The less you think to move
Quicker you are truly moving
Lesser is great, I assure you Lesser
force you may apply unlimited
universes you can reach.

Luanda, April 4, 2021

Love is a narrative; love is a story.

5.TIME OF TRANSITION

Nations welcome the
fragile for what seems
eternal.
Clouds of the dark are
clearing.
I salute your time of transition.
I bow to your ancient rotation.

Presence scrolls in
absence. Distance swims to
transit.
The second extends its might.
The year paints in lonesomeness.
I praise you, the transit of
liberation when the minute crosses
the need.

6.MY LIFE

My life started with a deep sleep.
Nine months was deep formation.
My trip started with a deep breath.
You ushered my dream to this reality.

…wish I could decide on my race.
…wish I could choose my origins.
…wish I could rewrite my future.
…wish I could choose my news.

My life is a dream, I am still asleep.
My life is a journey, I am still walking.
In your bosom I find meaning.
My dream is to interpret dreams.
In your matrix I find covering.
Like a motion picture, my life moves. In
the speed of the wind, I dream as I talk.
My life is the unknown of knowledge.
Let me see it again, I ask you to rewind.
You can see, my life is a written decision.

My life is a purpose hidden in the cloud. I wish I could reach higher, read - me here. I wish I could sit and relax, watch - it again. My life is a covenant sealed in the atom of grain. My life is a chapter in the book of written grace.

…wish - I could choose my parents.
…wish - I could choose my mentor.
…wish - I could choose my death.
…wish - I could choose my land.
…wish - I could choose my destiny.
…wish - I could choose my life.
…wish - I could live forever.

Follow the gift in the person, not the person in the gift.
You are not what you drive, but what drives you

7. WHO IS MY READER

Who is my reader?
My reader is my guest.
In the secret of quantum host,
He welcomes me.
As an instructor or tractor in the sector of her golden mind,
She listens to me,
as a minister or tax collector.

Who is my reader?
My reader is my leader.
Who is my reader?
My reader is my follower, my redeemer.
Transport me from writer to author, messenger.
Elevate me from speaker to preacher, immortal.
Promote me from player to director, instructor.

My reader is my uncle.
My reader is my anchor.
In the dark street of his solitude, altitude.
He accepts me as a brother or follower,

In the cold corner of his addiction or condition.

He sings along with me as an inmate or soul
mate, Fights with me, his muscles brown,
wrestler.
Read me, with her avid eyes, full of tears, lawyer.
Who is my reader?
My reader is my listener.
In his mental imagery he scans me between lines.
He portrays me as a storyteller or fortune-teller.
Scrutinizes me between my lines as an inspector.

Who is my reader?
My reader is my provocateur.
Who is my reader?
My reader is my challenger.
My reader is my mother.
My reader is my motor.

If you can read, you can lead.

8. LAY DOWN

Lay Down.
You are a baby, you cannot sit.
You cannot stand, you can
walk.

Lay down.
You are tired, you need to rest.
You need a nap, you need to
sleep.

Lay down.
You are sick, you need to heal.

Lay down.
You find love.
You are laying down a foundation.
Lay down to download love and
peace. Lay down after a long walk to
wealth.

Lay down.
You are old, you are going.
Lay down to depart from this world.

Lay down to leave your body.
Lay down to live in the spirit.
Lay the foundation of eternity.
You came laying down.
You will survive laying down.
You will depart from the earth laying down.

Portland, Maine.
April 17, 2018

9. WHERE AM I FROM?

I am from the beach,
near the high hills of Muizenberg.
I am from Vilakazi Street,
walking with the mighty.

I breathe from the breeze which blows from Robben
island. My father's dream is peace.
Here I am,
speaking for the lonely.
You are dying to know where I am from.
I am from Africa.

I am from the Cape of Good Hope, where two oceans embrace.
I am from the land of Melodies, where Rolihlahla Mandela
rests. I swim electrically to the sea, navigating to a better land.
My master teaches me harmony.
Here you are, speaking about differences.
You are living to know where I am from.
I am from Malaika.

I am from the Inga Falls, resting on the feet of the mighty
Kongo. I am from the high peaks of Virunga,
         where uranium ushered Nagasaki.
I am from the rainforest, where you breathe London, in East
London.
Yes, I am from the land of Cortham, where Lumumba rests in acid.
You are living to know where I am from.

I am from the Berlin Conference.
I am from the longitude desert of the Namib,
    from the salty pans of Etosha.
I am from the valley of Kasanje,
  where greatness divorces popularity.
I am from the land of Welwitschia,
    where reality meets universality.
I am from the land of the brave,
    where braver ushers victory.
I am from the silence of dunes,
  meditating on the divine designer.

I am from the River Okavango,
 where Apere walked crossing the odds of
 adversity. …where inner said it is impossible.
…where my fish became my meat.
You are crying to know my philosophy
You want to know where I am from.
I am from the belly of Windhoek.

Windhoek West, December 5, 2013
In memory of Nelson Rolihlahla Mandela

10.KILL MY PAINKILLER

After time I realize,
My pain made me so
wise. After cry I fantasize,
My praise can win a
fight. After touching my
heart, My faith made me
fly.

You call me, I will follow. I
am standing for your love.
After miles into the dark,
I am hoping for your light.

If I am the last to be helped,
You'll be the first to give me
help. If I am weak sometimes,
You are strong every time. If I
need love in my life,
You so love in my heart.

You call me, I will
follow. I am living by

faith.
If I am ready to live for
you. I am ready for
sacrifice.

Kill my painkiller.
Teach me to know.
You are the great, I Am.
Take my pain away.
Teach me to stand.
In your presence,
Resurrect my life again.
Help me to live my dream again.

After tough times in the past,
My pain turned into praise.
After long way in the dust,
My pain turns into dance.
After touching your
garment, The lamb that was
slain.

Full of worries and full of
sorrow, My dream seems to
fade.
After time in to the mud,
My redeemer came with grace.

Kill my painkiller.
Teach me to know.
You are the great, I Am
Take my pain away.
Touch me to stand.
In your presence,
Resurrect my faith.
Master, lead me to know you better.

11. CALL ME

Call me to sing, call me to testify,
about the woman on the shake.
Call me to speak, call me to magnify,
about her strength in times of rain.
Call me to not miss her phone call,
She is ready for the race.
Call me to teach her some courses,
I want to stand her for love.

Help me to give, help me to edify,
a bridge for a child crossing the lake
Help me to give, help me to glorify,
her strength in the time of pain.
Help me not miss her call for hope,
She may be ready for the song.
Help me to teach her one note.
I want to plan for her moment.

Choose your class, be intelligent,

choose your master, be wise.

12 .LET'S GO BRUSH OUR TEETH

That was the last thing I was prepared to hear.
I managed to brush my teeth at the bus terminal.
I brushed my teeth in the shower upon arrival.
I checked all my teeth and breath to survive the first
kiss, Just in case.
Not something of dry lips touching hairy faces.

Let us brush our teeth came as a shortcut introduction to intimacy. A
pin code deduction of chemistry.
The code of charming hormonal fasting.
You will not unlock the lips of the nurse,
without brushing your teeth
When all hope vanished and all trials left,
the sound of her voice echoed the dark/
You want to kiss,
then let us go brush our teeth.
The rest has grown up to become history

.

13.PRAISE UNDER PAIN

Celebrate your birth and rejoice.
Remember the pain you caused.
You were born causing mum
tears.
We praise and give you a
name. From pain came the
praise.
Find a switch and switch it
on. When pain hits your
brain,
sing and dance for glory.
March right to the human you,
From humiliation came elevation.

Read and roll your tears on, When
education calls you crazy. Listen to
the lecture of nature. Urge the drain
as rain walks on wet. From
hardship came the worship

Praise under pain for reverence.
Praise under pain for eloquence.
Praise under praise for
relevance. Praise under pain for
excellence.

From hardship came, the worship
From humiliation came the
elevation From pain came the praise
From the test came the testimony.

14.SOMETIMES

Sometimes I feel lonely.
Sometimes I am lost.
Your grace made me strong,
everybody seems to know.

Your love seals my feelings.
Your grace leads my
thoughts. Some battles have
been lost.
Every war has been won.

Sometimes I feel empty.
Sometimes I am low.
Your voice makes me sing.
Your return seems too long.

Your love makes me move.
Your faith leads my work.
Some battles have been lost.
However, your song has been written,
marching close to the lamb,
moving strong through my faith.
I may be moving so slow,
But I am not going backward.
New dance to land.
Kalunga called my name.

I can touch your garment,
moving me,
praising your name.

Some friends are
running. When times are
cold,
Your word keeps me walking.
Every moment you seem
close. Your love seals my
offering. Your hope leads to
my work. Some battles have
been gone. Every war has
been crowned.

Now Fake is Fashion

15. AFRICAN BEAT

Kudikudakudikuda
Kudidikuda
Kukidkudakuda
Kudikuda
Kudidikuda

It is so dark, I cannot see my shadow.
The candle just melted in the meadow.
The somber welcomes my window. The
night is dark - black, but not blind. My
heartbeat will synchronize to the beat.

Kudikudakudikuda
Kudidikuda
Kukidkudakuda
Kudikuda

Beat by beat, I am getting to the vibe,
harmonizing and downloading my lyrics.
Tap-tap, tambour of skin,
Brown, wood tabour of fire
Dance dance, sounds of Africa
The music of land of the dark,
the tambour rolling.
Sense not my beat.

Read not my timing.
Profound my yes, is my sense of combinedness.
Perfumed me dark, is the skin of my romance.
Hips moving me from Sahara to Kilimanjaro;
'Bring me back my Dakar,
Restore my pride.

Stop me from visiting Thando; her touch says Gugulethu.

Harass me not to meet Zola; his voice sings Kalahari. My Sister
is in love with Shilongo, his mantel covers Timbuktu. My brother
likes Ndombolo, her moves connect Antananarivo. Welcome to
the nation of rainfalls, harmonize me with Mambazo.

16. THE TIME OF THE TIMES

Tiling for the times, building on the line.
Edifying the path, intersection of your life.
Minimizing for the fight, pacifying on the ground.
Exploring ropes - mild intervention of sound.

Time of the times, learning from your past.
Time of the future, pacifying on the ground.
Time of the moment, coloring your trust.
Time of the unknown, understanding your vice.

Playing on the path, regulating from the sight A safe game
in temple flesh, collecting your breath. A mockery of
blessings, bush-burning and cracking. The slaughters of
the lamb, bombs exploding on your face.

Time of the times, gaming with the mice.
Time of the future, spacing for the lost.
Time of the moment, talking with the wise.
Time of the unknown, watering on the rock.

Timing of the till, designing through the gap.
Speaking of hope, judging from the place.
Walking all day long, thinking on the step.
Dreaming on the floor, meditating on the

base. Writing for the soul, singing to the land. Time of the times, on the melody of your life. Time of the future, on the soliloquy of your mind. Time of the moment, on the symphony of your art Time of the unknown, on the cacophony of your march.

Better a crazy dream than no dream.

Knowing too much does not know so much.

17. MAN OF PAIN

Man of pain you are.
Many are standing on my
way. Many put doubt on my
faith.
They cannot stop me - to love you.
They cannot stop me - to serve you.
They cannot stop me - to follow
you.

Man of pain you are.
Your pain taught me to
praise. Your pain taught me
to wait.
Hardship leads me to worship.
Hardship leads me to know you.
Hardship leads me to follow
you.

Man of pain you are.
Tears are falling on my cheeks. Tears
are falling on your hand. They can
help me - to learn from you. They
can raise me - to stand for you. They
can heal me - to grow for you

Man of pain you are.

Many are working on my case. Many
are waiting for me to fail. They cannot
stop me - to work for you. They
cannot stop me - to sing for you They
can help me - to know you more.
Man of pain you are.
Wind is blowing on my ten.t
Drought is knocking on my shake.
That cannot stop me - to help for you
That cannot stop me - to save for you
That cannot stop me - to honor you

Your shortcut to popularity is compromise; your shortcut to greatness is sacrifice.

Bad is low and quick, good is high and slow.

Greatness is not cheap

18.HIS AND HER POSSIBLE

His possible trance,
Transcending.
Watering our possible,
Moving.
Her possible walk,
Longing.
Wavering our dove,
Steps crawling.
Dust mixed feeling,
For the orphan seeking.

Core mystery,
Mere tormenting.
Polishing our poetry,
Tourmaline.
Close mystery tears,
Palavering.
Featuring our millions,
Dreaming.
Task rude Kick
Tambouring,
For the organ sick of playing.

His active walk,

Sweating.

Rolling our mountain,

Sliding.

Her possible pain,

Shaving.

Waxing our low bread

Preaching

Crowd fool, mild clapping,

For the prophet still sobbing.

Confess, report and bless your partner often and your relationship will become a life partnership.

Love is so expensive that money cannot afford it.

19. THERE MUST BE SOMEONE

There must be someone somewhere,
Looking for me.
There must be someone somewhere,
Watching on me.
There must be someone somewhere.
There must be someone on my way.

There must be someone in space,
Calling my name.
There must be some out there,
Reading my poem.
There must be someone somewhere.
There must be someone on my way.

There must be someone in some place,
Leading my way.
There must be someone in some land,
Looking on me.
There must be someone somewhere.
There must be someone on my way.
There must be someone somewhere,
More clever than me.
There must be someone somewhere,
Wiser than me.
There must be someone somewhere.

There must be someone on my way.

There must be someone
somewhere, Stronger than me.
There must be someone somewhere,
Holier than me.
There must be someone somewhere.
There must be someone on my way.

20. AFRICA WETU

Africa wetu zizwe za bantu
basakumunua
kala munkembo, nkosi za bantu
kotele mu engipito

One day, I see you crying.
Another day, I see you
shining. One way, I see you
crawling.
Another way, I see you
learning. One side, I see you
flying.

Africa wetu, wetu, wetu, wetu
Africa Wetu zizwe za bantu
basakumunua
Kala munkembo, nkosi za
bantu kotele mu engipito

In my dreams, I see you fighting. Coz'
you follow, I know you are worthy. In
his name, commend the morning. Coz'
you my land claiming victory. In my
dreams, I see you winning.
Africa wetu, wetu, wetu, wetu

By the riverside of Limpopo,
By the riverside of the Longo,
By the lake side of
Tanganyika, By the desert side
of Namibia, I can see that you
are worthy.

21. WHEN YOU HAVE NOTHING

When you have nothing,
It looks like you are nothing.
When you have nothing,
the sky looks hanging.
When you have nothing,
friends start questioning.
Your bank bangs on your ears, as
if you are about to explode. Money
seems not to grow on trees, your
confidence is tested.
Your hope may vanish.

When you have nothing,
it does not mean you are nothing.
When you have nothing,
God becomes everything.
When you have nothing,
your child thinks you have everything.

When you have nothing,
Your dream may run slow.
When you have nothing,
Your wisdom may look like falsity.
When you have nothing,

All things look wavering.
Your knowledge of the deep,
may focus on the superficial butter.
When you have nothing,
it does not mean you can do
nothing. When you have nothing,
God becomes everything.

When you have nothing,
You forgot that you came with
nothing When you have nothing,
You forgot that you would take
nothing When you have nothing,
You may think your neighbor misses nothing.
When you have nothing,
You may think money is everything.

When you have nothing,
they may think you are not
worthy. When you have nothing,
God becomes everything.

When you have nothing,
Remember the air is everything
When you have nothing,
remember life is something.
When you have nothing,
remember love is everything.

When you have nothing,
remember faith is everything.
When you have nothing,
remember nothing is not nothing.
When you have nothing, God
can provide for everything.

22. AFRICAN APATHY

Maybe the mix of Hollywood Bollywood, not the
right diet for a movie addict and crook. Maybe the
mix of Facebook, Twitter, and Google, will not
digest my proverbial diatonic voice. I became slow
to hunt, to create and resolve. I became slow to
prevent, project, analyze, and think. I went from
couch potato, to couch tomato. This is not me.
I am a runner, and I am an African marathon.

Maybe the mix of touch screen and smartphone do
not work on my dialectic communication. Maybe
the combination of innovation and tradition do not
fit in my traditional motivation of education. I
became a quick-fix fixer, a quick money seeker. I
became a fast-food solution, a quick gratification. I
became a facelift manipulator, a drum vibratory. I
was downgraded from doctor to witchdoctor, from
prophet to fortune teller.

Maybe the mix of democracy and socialism,
did not find its way in my sociology; Niber-Africanist.
Maybe the mix of capitalism, Marxism, and liberalism,
did not work in my monarchic, backyard leadership. I
became a political humanoid, a leadership undertaker.
I went from freedom fighter, to freedom supervisor.

Here I am,
looking like a proletariat zombie - a fear-seller, Spitting
blood upon the values that I fought ready to die. African
apathy that rejected the old woman's wisdom African
apathy that sold my uncle to the altar of slavery. African
apathy that lavished my mother's dark skin light. African
apathy that crushed my daughter's hope for Africa.

23. LOOK AT THE WINDOW

The future is coming.
By the window it is closing.
The present is going to pass.
Keep faith, keep hope, and
pray. The past brought here,
as the present is taking us there.

Look at the window and see, healing
is coming and love is close. We are in
the school of healing. Look at the
window and see wellness.

The door may be shut down.
Tears have been falling down.
At a certain time you feel
down. We have heard about
hardships.
This was built on our impossible.
You are sitting on what they
build. It is time to write your
story.
At the window see the unlimited.
Hold on to your black ink
bottle. Take your white plain

paper, look at the window and
write. Look at the window and
fly. And don't forget to breathe.
You are a window escaper -
door closes as a window opens.

24.WHO CAN LIVE HERE

Who can survive here?
The air that we breathe smells of blood and
anarchy. The water that you drink tastes of fear
and lies. You should not say what you think and
live.
You are living in a time where fake is fashionable.

Who can win here?
Your victory does not depend on your strength and
wisdom. Your victory depends on the desecration of a
referee. The ground that you fight for, is slippery and risky.
The cause that you seek, is bloody and tricky.

Who can lead here?
Your vision is blinded by greed and hypocrisy. The
mission you are on, is full of ambush and lethargy, your
message rejected before it comes out of your heart. The
soil you tread is full of personal mines and dynamite

Who can pray and be holy here?
Your faith legalized, according to an ideological
agenda. Your God only accepts, if He fits into their
temple. Your act of worship is effective, if it fits into
their idol. Your inspiration is right, when it suits their
aspirations.
Who can make a difference here?
Designed to be different, to make a difference. The
anointing on you will break the yokes of idolatry.
Your God stands near you, you understand near him.
Your life is a mission, your mission is possible.

Who said you would lose here?
They are lost in illusion, lost in material separatism.
They could not see the serpent becoming a python.
You saw it before it came, you said visionary. They
have the dream without interpretation - fiction.
Called to lose to win.
They are just winning to lose.

Huambo, Angola.
November 16, 2014

25. NOT FAR, CLOSER

My Savior coming no longer,
to finish and flourish what He built in
me, worship and hardship, I wept.
…enough to water Namib and
Sahara, I dry up to the core of my
well.
Suddenly I smell His perfume.

My Master is coming closer.
All of my pain became nothing. Enemies
are crying, friends are rejoicing. Lord,
you are near, so close that I feel. Not
enough of you Savior, lovingly. When I
thought it all over and off, you rang the
bell of my call.
On my voice it is rolling,
not perfectly but moving.

Carpenter, I got your calling,
To build in your House.
I came to the wedding Looking for love.
My Redeemer I cannot wait,
To fall into your arms.

Secret lover, as I have been
waiting for water to change into
wine.
My Mentor, coming so
closer, to lead my halo on
fire,
Not far, closer.
My Savior is waving so near, closer. I
was too tired to be tired, breathing.
Beat by beat, I got to the pointless,
on my resistant, senseless vile.
Suddenly the friend that stood, came.

Huambo, Angola 22 November 2014

26. THE DAY I DECIDED NOT TO FIGHT

The day I decided not to fight xenophobia,
you just insulted my mother,
Stripped her dignity.

The day I decided to walk the road of peace, not to
kill, You just waxed my sister,
your love cut short her inspiration.

On the day I decided not to fight racism,
you just spit upon my father's skin,
Humiliated him, locked his prejudices.

My calling reminded all transporters,
my vision dismayed all, my message said it all,
My mission.

The day I decided not to fight stigma
You just denied my best friend the opportunity to live
peacefully, You killed her for ideology.

My blood type said it all, fighter.
My heart pumped it all, winner.
My coach said it all, overcomer.
My God said it all, conqueror.
The day I decided not to fight manipulation

You stole my pride and corrupted my mind.
You took me back to the fight, at the core fire of spiritual warfare.

My spirit said it all, achiever.
My destiny said it clear, trailblazer.
My bones remind you, believer.
My faith said it all, transformed.

27. WHAT SEEMS ELEVATED

What seems elevated?
You put not trust in.
Nevertheless, put your trust in what seems
humiliated. Learn through elevated humiliation,
through patience, long-suffering and
consistency. Pray, pray to the God of time,
The father of the result.

What seems elevated?
What seems rejected, inner and outer.
Applaud you in another self.
Much is done in lower garage,
From higher and effective, elevation of grace

What seems elevated, root is.
What seems elevated, deep goes.
What seems elevated, hunger went.
What seems elevated, humiliated was.

28. I AM NOT THE POET

I am not the poet.
I am not telling a story.
I am not putting pictures out there.
Less than that, I am trembling,
trembling with words - babbling,
babbling in my uneducated brain.

I do not know what to call it,
Song or prose, psalm or
prayer. I have no story to tell.
I have no words to say.

You are silent.
I am in silence.
I am not the poet.
I am not a poetry maker.

29. SOLDIER OF THE UNKNOWN

Right awake, your tank is filling up slowly,
As if your night was not so hot, thirsty.
You rolled at night, sweating to death.
You prayed for rain, any of that fresh air. Your
night was another fight, a fight for sleep. On
the rumble of truth, your soul will win. In the
battleship of love, your heart is a winner. In
the war against lies, your actions say truth.
Train to win over manipulations.

Soldier of the cross, we salute you, we love
you. In the dark, you wonder if you will make
it. You tried to sleep at night and work the day
shift. Not a sleep warrior, you cannot rest.
Your nights are moated, your hut a
battlefield. The enemy steps around, ready
to strike us. In the fight for peace, your
destiny seals us.
On the rumble of faith, you are an overcomer. In the
struggle for justice, you protected us, innocent.
On the way to Holocaust, you took up for our lives.
Soldier of faith, we salute you, we shall not forget. We
know you are not rich, but you can reach out. We know
you are not holy, but your commander is. We know you

are weak, but life made you a hero. We know you are not
an eagle, but you can fly higher. Soldier of the unknown,
we shall testify your deeds, yes. Evil shall not prevail, as
long as you are with us. Assailants will not walk free, as
long as you are our judge.

Corruption will not lead, as long as you are our
friend. Idol worship will perish, as long as you
lead.

Soldier of light, your tears washed away our dusty coast.
We know your pain - what you have to bear, to save. We
know your humiliation - what you have learned, to gain.
We know how many enemies you must kill to heal. We
have been there, under the mercy of the rough. Soldier of
heaven, you stretched out your hand, and saved.

30 .AFRICAN CROSS

I made up my mind to live or die by faith.
Not through faith, nor justice of second
hope. My hope is that justice and happiness
come. Not through fear or bloody
aspirations. I hope Makelele will stay milky,
not bloody.

African cross, the wood of my ebony tears.
African cross, the limitation of my ideas.
African cross, the mortification of my past.
African cross, the slaughter of my generation.
African cross, I decided to carry it to the
forest.

I made up my mind to lead twelve disciples.
Through knowledge not through ignorance. My
son said, "Master, focus on sowing your seed." I
said, "as long as there will be rain and water, seeds
planted and Lukunga will water me."

African cross, the riot of the poor angry.
African cross, the revolver of the weak.
African cross, the massacre of the no name.
African cross, the policies of the lost
winner. African cross, the darkness of our

wisdom.
I made up my mind to love and speak life,
Not lies, not truth, no minutes, no report.
Where most of our lonely desks teach us to run,
I believe in seeking and walking the lonely
Calvary, Carrying my wood heavy, black African
Cross

African cross, the helper that reached out to my kin. African cross, the nurse that was near my birth. African cross, the editor of my prophetical papyrus. African cross, African cross, the politics of emotion motionless. African cross, the football of goalkeeping not reaching.

Luanda, Angola 19 Jan 2015

31. SAY IT LOUDER

Say it loud again, that you choose me,
when my enemy says it low.
Call it a life, a mere stamp of a dream.
Look at your eyes, my tears are rolling.
My foes will not understand why,
when you love this dream of loving me.
Bring up my mocker to choose life not death. Let the one
that seeks my elimination be mute. Judge them on the blood
of Octavio Fernando.
On the dream of Martin Luther King Jr, I will
pray. For David had sung the same song for life.
I will stand for real, and then I may understand that truth.
Smoke and fire on my bones cracking, fuming. Strangling my
intestines, I cannot breathe at the place - the place of my dream, the
dream of Nelson Mandela.
I was born at a place of selling breath, selling water
- Market full of thirsty black hearts, crying for light.
My foes are expecting me to shut down and be silent.
Let us pick up the pieces of that dream that slipped.
Let us wake up to the blood of those who have
fallen, For the same fight, for spirit and truth.
Let us not faint in front of the wrath of bulldogs/ Let's
remind ourselves that we are still dreamers. We were
born for a time like this, time of the dreamer.

Living is Moving.

32. MOVING ME STILL

It is moving in me, a sort of vibration,
steam, moving in me, kind of motion of
claim,
purely conversation, monologue of birth,
for the past decades, it has been here in me.

I am trying to shut it up, down still
moving. I tried to lock it down, but it was
still panoramic.
It is walking in me, barefoot kissing my bones. It
is crawling in me, fast-food burning my tongue.

Curly scalp, translation of chronology to save. For the
last forty-two seconds, it has been there beating. I
never forgot its vibrant touch, growing old in me. I
learned to bend it up. Mystery of the unknown.

It is clear, a monologue of dichotomy, mythology. It is the real, momentum of Carthage, monopoly. This is the rule of Memphis, waves of Nile, Niger. I tried not to resist its mighty wind from the belly, Tunis.

At the end of the move, we should not stand still. The move is here, in my chromosomes, stealth. In addition, nothing will be crazy. At the end of the trip, I may fall, flawlessly arriving.

33. AS WE THINK

And the mercy of God,
We are not as clean as we think.

And the will of God,
We are not as ready as we think.

And the time of God,
We are not waiting as we could.

And the glory of God,
We are not as humble as we think.

And the word of God,
We are not as wise as we think.

And the spirit of God,
We are not as spiritual as we think.

And the Kingdom of God, We
are not united, as we believe.

34. MONEY ME NOT

So quickly my conversation with
you changed so quickly as your tone
stinks. I could smell your real
motive,
for traveling miles and smiles.

Money me not, the altar of my inspirations.
Money me not, the standards of my
aspiration. Money me not, the secret of my
motivation. Money me not, the causes behind
my mission.

So intensely ready to sell.
Whatever comes to your mind for gain?
Money me not, I have dignity, pride. I
suffer at times, to get what you seek.

Money me not, for the altar of my message.
Money me not, on the lane of my vision.
Money me not, the essence of my elevation.
Money me not, a conviction of my
information.

It is like any business, you said.
I do not believe in mercantilism, all for
gain. I stood for change, liberation and
charity. For the gift I received, no price
can force.
Money me not, on the stone of my
transformation. Money me not, on the route of
my motion. Money me not, on the format of my
formation. Money me not, on the root of my
vocation.

So slow, I learn to give, to lay down.
Whatever comes on my way, I sacrifice?
I travel miles to find this gold.
This is verticality, enlaced with immortality.

Money me not, on the altar of my humiliation.
Money me not, on the tomb of my
resurrection. Money me not, on the speed of
my rotation. Money me not, on the rock of
translation.

40.SPEAK TO ME

Speak to me; wake me tall,
in the diminish of the might.
Talk to us; shake my soil,
on my mother's speechless night,
on conversation of the monks,
for emulator of the crown,
In the motivation of the tough
by the transformation of the bound.

Speak to me directly.
Distribute me on the bronze.
Talk to me deep, by the diction of logos.
Mold me to the silence of your throne. Think
with me, with a dissertation of logic. Speak to
me, when glory and fame stand still.

When I can see words, voyages,
there I can touch your hot,
languages, from who logic recall
salvages,
my thoughts speak to me in carnage. Use me,
drag me quickly on the pages. My time is
spelling, is spelling you, interlocutor. I may not

live long, smooth verbal montages.

Grab me to you, envelop me with your vocabulary.

You are a dictation from the dictionary of compassion. I am
listening to your conjugations, lawyer of the immigrants.

Conjugate me real, punctuate my ink, advocate for the
refugees. Use inflammations of folly, poetry, and mystery,
leader of the landless.

Speak to my past, read my future,

change my misery of asylum seeking.

Lose my present; change my past,

from the homology of losing my village

Let the fouls think that they are wiser than you are; it is the best way to teach them the difference between wisdom and foolishness.

41. MORE THAN THAT

You are more than what you have.
You are more than what you are looking
for. You are more than the color of your
skin. You can fly above your physical
limitations. If you can read, you can lead.
You are more than that.

You are more than your salary.
You are more than your bank account. It is not
what you have that sustains who you are.
However, who you are, produces what you have.
If you can be, you can become.
You are more than that.

You were born without clothes.
Your mother's hands covered your
skin. You were born hungry,
mother's milk was there for you.
The air was stored at your disposal.
Your need was covered, and here you are.

42. NOTHING IS STILL

You are not blind, but there is no light.
What you don't see, sees you in the dark.
Your dream knows your destination.
It is better to have a crazy dream, than no dream.
There is seed of possibility within the impossible,
Most of the crazies of yesterday, are the wise of
today Nothing is still; everything is translating.

If you can stand, you can understand.
If you can remove it, you can move.
Your humiliation is carrying your elevation. Your
disappointment will bring your appointment. Remember
the process is more important than the result. If you can
believe, you can live.
Nothing is still, everything is rotating.

You are not managing time, Your time is managing
you. The right time is now; this is your time.
Your hardship will lead you to worship.
Your pain is designing your praise.
Nothing is still, everything is vibrating.

43. ONE BRAVE IS ENOUGH

You made a choice and you trusted me with your soul. You cast your vote in my direction.

As you sacrificed your time, the sun shined.

As you offered your love, your soul broke.

I recorded all your prayers, I archived all your petitions. One brave person is enough to save our souls from the grave.

You are brave to face the bees of my honey.

You displayed bravery, in the face of mockery.

You demonstrated mastery, in the face of robbery.

Your hand reached me in the pit of deprivation.

I shall stand to confess, I will understand to profess. One brave is enough to save the land of the brave.

When many are confused, you turn self-confidence to self-esteem. You humbled yourself and walked the narrow way of faith. Many confused the gift in the hero and the hero in the gift. You stood alone in the battle of solitude and manipulation.

As you swallow your bitter tisane, your infirmity heals. I will guide you to the hills, I will lead you to the dream. One brave person is enough to save our families from famine.

One brave is enough to save the land of the brave. One brave is enough to turn the impossible to possible. One brave person is enough to change our stagnation to rotation. One brave is enough to translate our doubt to faith. One brave is enough to transform our deformation to formation. One brave person is enough to move us from nightmare to dream. One brave person is enough to edit our manuscript to become a script. One brave is enough to save the land of the brave.

44. DON'T BE AFRAID

Do not let your faith fade in the dark.
Do not let your time pass in the sight.
Do not be afraid to fail, do not be afraid to lose.
The earth rounds, the wind is blowing.
Polish your music, arrange your notes.
Your conductor is directing your symphony.

Spread your wings, be bold - keep your smile, be
wise. Human response will not determine your result.
Be strong, save your strength, write your music.
Do not look at your enemies' celebration.
We have been in this before, we were here before.
Read the time, be on time, and lead on time.

When fear comes, wait, and time your movement.
When you are scared, breathe, and change your
direction. When you are afraid, give time to the tempo.
When you are afraid, call a friend and pray.
When you are scared, breathe your fear out of your soul.

When Your body says you are going to fail, say, "I am ready."
When your prediction says you are going to lose, say, "I am
ready." Revolutionaries make mistakes, as mistakes make
revolutionaries. Be bold, and refuse to be afraid for the sake of
being afraid. Be courageous, because you will live once, and die
once.

45. SHOW ME THE COLD

Show me the cold!
I did not know what this was all about.
As we say, "I feel cold" you say, "I am cold."
I didn't know how the cold could hurt.
Until I became one of them;
I became homeless among them.

Show me the cold!
Do not show it to my mother.
She always fancies winters abroad.
She doesn't know how it hurts her son. Because
she said, "send me the snow pictures." Then I
slid, falling upon it and broke my screen. I
became homeless, the cold became my blanket.

Show me the cold!
Show it to my friends from shelters.
When we faced the below zero to be
heroes. When Fahrenheit and Celsius
became allies. That moment you need just a
cup of survey,
I did not know what winter is all about, Until I
landed here homeless, but not hopeless.

Portland, Maine. Winter 2018

46. I DARE YOU TO SAY IT

I dare you to say it,
Say it from your heart.
Say it again.
Say it in the dark, it will be light.

Say it to death, it will be life. Say it
to the poor, wealth will come. Say
it to the sick doctors, heal them.
Say it again and again.

Say it to the lost preachers, find
them. Say it to the present, bring the
future. Say it when you are blind.
Say it again, produce fireworks.

Say it to reap love, and love
more. Say it when you feel or
want to. Say it again until you
can.
I dare you to say, "I love you."

December 22, 2017
Orlando, Florida

47. PURE MAGIC

There is a reason to believe in a
creator, when you see this.
There is reason to believe in the
divine. when you witness this.

There is pure magic in the snow,
when you walk upon the snow.
There is a reason to preserve
health, when you touch this.

There is a reason to sow love,
when you experience this.
There is pure magic,
when you come across the snow.

There is a reason of purity,
when you smell the snow.
There is a reason for
innocence, when you taste the
snow.

There is pure magic in the snow,
when black tries to surf on the
snow. There is a pure motion,
when you walk on the snow

48. I WILL WALK

On the steps of those in silence,
I will walk.

Upon the tears of the rejected,
I will walk.

Flying upon the resistance of the
ungodly, swimming against the tide of
the unwise, I walk!

Head swinging, breath shortening,
I am walking.

Surely, the destiny closes the gap,
I am approaching in the dark of the city of light
, I will walk.

In the place of mortification,
I stand.

I cannot feel my heartbeat, I can feel the
wind. I am the target of a moving bullet.
I must walk.

I will walk,
as I am walking.

49. THEIR SPIRIT LEADS ME

In addition, suddenly the village got hot and
dark, Hot in the deep dark.
I was not walking into better future
Maybe I was, and suddenly I was lost in despair
The ruins of my spirit, they appeared.
I was demoted in the deep, darker.
Soon doors of hell start opening and closing.
Nevertheless, I was being led.
Their spirit was leading me.

"Slave, slave,"
I have heard their voices singing.
I just discovered I was one of them.
One with them, among them,
Son of them.

"Slave, slave,"
Slave in my own land, slave for nothing.
I cried for freedom, I cried for support.
The voice of my predecessors came unto my soul,
"Follow, follow us to the other side of the ocean."
Their spirit was leading me

"Slave, slave,"

Where are the aches of my ancestors, the remains of my elders? I am living free at last, free in the land of the free. I am at the place of their arrival.

50. THE CREATOR DECIDED

I looked again at the picture of his last
march, His face covered with uncertainty.
I listened to his last speech.
His feet were shaking,
same as today, the sky is crying.

It recalls the day that the dream shook -
one day, where we had to go,
one shot, of one bullet ending.

I am looking at the picture again,
as we say it again and again -
when a prophet has to die,
"He knew it, he knew it was coming."

He knew that was the last day
He knew that was the last day of the fight.

He was resisting, but his master recalled
him. He wanted to fight, again - resist more.
The creator decided to pass the torch to us. The creator
decided to pass the dream to us. The creator decided
that thirty-nine years were enough.

Portland, Maine. April 4, 2018 - In memory of MLK 50
Politics is an art of policies and politeness.

Lies will sing in your mind; truth will sink in your spirit.

51. SNOW VERTICAL

The alarm of my smoky kitchen
woke me up from waiting on.
I run to open door to breathe,
vertically falling white greeted me,
Some kind of white, mystery
powder.

Silently and vertically floating around, I
recorded a short video to remember. I
called Instagram, consulted Facebook.
My WhatsApp reminded me to share. My
social media surely was tweeting.

After many years, finally we met -
falling in harmony in front of me. Many
had experienced that before. Not like I
could imagine snow inspiring, finally
given the baptismal vertical touch

Westbrook, Maine. November 13, 2017
witnessing my first snow

52. I AM FROM AFRICA

I am not a Congolese,
Coz' I don't know the meaning of it. I am a
Gongo, grandson of the Mani Congos. Nzinga
Nkuwu, NsakuDivunda, Ne Kongo, Kings of
Kongo Kingdom of MbazaKongo, The capital
of KongoDiantotila in Africa, Where the
Majestic River Kongo designed me. The river
is in Africa, it is an African river,
Therefore I am from Africa.

I am not Angolan,
Coz' I don't know what it means.
I grew up in the city of Luanda,
of the kingdom of Ngola Kiluanji.
Luanda means, beat him up in Kikikongo.
Beaten by time and circumstances,
but king Ngola wasn't an Angolan,
was a friend and brother of the king of
Kongo. Both leaders and kings in Africa,
Therefore, I am from Africa.
I am not what is on the passport.
It is just how the dictators directed it.
I am not what is on my birth certificate.

It is what the cold war decided for me.
I never had a chance to vote, they voted for me.
I never had a chance to speak, to think aloud.
They took away my language, my culture, my Kongo.

They did not take Africa out of me.
They did not succeed in destroying MbazaKongo.

I am not a French speaker.
I learned French to voice my concerns,
to send my plea further.
I am not an English speaker, I learned it to brainstorm with you,
For you to understand me.
I am a Kikongo speaker of idioms-that are more
African Moreover, vernacular is running in me.
Those languages are African languages,
Therefore I am an African, I am from Africa

Portland, Maine May 5, 2018.

53. THE "SHIT HOLE" MONOLOGUE

I was born and grew up in a "shit hole," nation that
produced Uranium to stop World War II. From the
"shit hole" village that provides Colthan, And
Cobalt for your cell phone and laptops.

I am from a "shit hole" city where Ali and Foreman fought,
called "rumble in the jungle."
I am from a "shit hole" land that brought
you, Nelson Mandela and Trevor Noah.
A "Shit hole" place,
where the ancestors of Martin Luther King Jr came from.

I am an inspirational Speaker and writer,
A singer and a thinker from a "shit hole"
background. I am from the "shit hole" continent,
where Jesus and parents sought asylum.
Following the path of my ancestors,
to interpret the American Dream.